IF JESUS CAME
TO MY HOUSE

BY

JOAN GALE THOMAS

Lothrop, Lee & Shepard Books
NEW YORK

FOR
MARGARET
ANGELINA

FOREWORD

It is easy to see why this unpretentious little book, originally published in England, has already sold 19 editions. Children have always liked stories with morals, and parents have always liked books with warmth and tenderness for their children. Perhaps it is this tenderness that is felt between the lines of the simple little verses together with the innocent artlessness of the illustrations that gives the book its rare and instant appeal.

Both text and pictures are identical with the British edition, except for the slight revisions that were made to adapt the book for American readers.

If Jesus came to my house
and knocked upon the door
I'm sure I'd be more happy
than I've ever been before.

If Jesus came to my house
I'd like Him best to be
about the age that I am
and about the height of me.

I'd run downstairs to meet Him,
the door I'd open wide,
and I would say to Jesus,
'Oh, won't you come inside?'

I'd offer Him my rocking chair,
—it's such a comfy seat—
and at the pleasant fireplace
He'd warm His little feet.

My kitten and my puppy dog
would sit beside His chair
and they would be as pleased as I
at seeing Jesus there.

Then I would put the kettle on
to make a cup of tea,
and we would be as happy
and as friendly as could be.

I'd show Him all the places
that are nicest in the house—
the hole behind the stairs
where I pretend that I'm a mouse.

The little window up above
where I can stand and see
the people passing down below
and yet they can't see me.

And then I think I'd show Him
the corner in the hall
where I'm sometimes rather frightened
by the shadows on the wall.

I always have to hurry
when I'm going past at night,
but hand in hand with Jesus
I'd be perfectly all right.

I'd show Him round the garden
and ask Him please to bless
the seeds that I have planted—
the peas and watercress.

And if the flowers I'd planted
were blooming on that day
I'd pick a bunch of all the best
for Him to take away.

Then while He held the basket
I would gather two or three
of the ripest rosy apples
from my special apple tree.

And all the little birds would come
and twitter up above
for joy at seeing Jesus
in the garden that they love.

And then we'd play with all my toys,
my nicest toys of course,
and He should have the longest ride
upon my rocking horse.

And with my bricks I'd build for Him
a palace of His own,
and He should be the little King
and sit upon the throne.

And when we'd done we'd stack the toys
all neatly on the shelf,
but first I'd let Him choose the best
and keep them for Himself.

And when at last the day was done
and shadows crossed the sky,
I'd see Him to the garden gate
and there we'd say goodbye,

And He'd perhaps say, "Thank you
for a lovely afternoon,"
and I would say, 'I do so hope
you'll come back very soon.'

And then He'd smile and wave goodbye,
and so would end our day—
but all the house would seem to smile
because He'd been our way.

I know the little Jesus
can never call on me
in the way that I've imagined—
like coming in to tea.

But I can go to His house
and kneel and say a prayer,
and I can sing and worship Him
and talk with Him in there.

And though He may not occupy
my cozy rocking chair,
a lot of other people
would be happy sitting there.

And I can make Him welcome
as He Himself has said,
by doing all I would for Him
for other folk instead.

And though the house is dark at night
with shadows on the wall,
I never need be frightened
when I'm going through the hall.

Although I cannot see Him
I still can feel Him near
to understand and hold my hand
and drive away my fear.

The flowers in my garden
He may not pick Himself,
but someone else would like them
upon his mantelshelf.

So if I know of any one
who's old or ill or sad
I'll take them there for Jesus's sake
and help to make them glad.

I still can share with Jesus
the nicest of my toys
by lending them or giving them
to poorer girls and boys.

And though He may not visit me
as I have wished He would,
yet even so He'll bless my house
if I am kind and good.